# GREAT
# CENTRAL
## from Nationalisation to Ratioı

Peter Waller

**UNIQUE BOOKS**

*Front cover:* Class V2 2-6-2 No 60831 seen near Aylesbury in 1959 at the head of the 'South Yorkshireman'.
*Marcus Eavis/Online Transport Archive*

*Previous page:* On 11 June 1961 Class B1 4-6-0 No 61271 passes under Bridge No 519 on the downward 1 in 176 gradient towards Brackley and Finmere with the 12.30pm service from Nottingham Victoria to Marylebone. Each of the three spans of the bridge was 55ft 6in. The bridge, which carried the B4525 over the railway, was some 435yd south of Helmdon station; the bridge still survives although there has been some infilling of the mile-long cutting in which it was situated.
*Mike Mitchell/Transport Treasury*

First published by Unique Books 2019
Reprinted 2020
© Text: Peter Waller 2019
© Photographs: As credited

ISBN: 978 0 9957493 6 8

A CIP record for this book is available from the British Library

Unique Books is an imprint of Unique Publishing Services Ltd, 3 Merton Court, The Strand, Brighton Marina Village, Brighton BN2 5XY.
www.uniquebooks.pub

Printed in the UK

**A note on the photographs**
Many of the illustrations in this book have been drawn from the collection of the Online Transport Archive, a UK-registered charity that was set up to accommodate collections put together by transport enthusiasts who wished to see their precious images secured for the long-term. Further information about the archive can be found at:
www.onlinetransportarchive.org or email
secretary@onlinetransportarchive.org

# INTRODUCTION

As part of the LNER, the Great Central's London Extension – the last of the great Victorian main lines to be completed – passed to the Eastern Region of British Railways on Nationalisation. Initially, under the new owners, it was very much business as usual.

Shortly before BR's take-over of the line, the LNER had, at the suggestion of Ronald Matthews, who was both chairman of the railway as well as being a former Master Cutler of the Company of Cutlers in Hallamshire, agreed that one return working from Sheffield – the 7.40am up service and the 6.15pm down service – should be named the 'Master Cutler'. It first operated in this guise on 6 October 1947. The train was known to staff as 'The Cutler' and, conveying a restaurant car in both directions, was general hauled by an 'A3' Pacific. A second named service – the 'South Yorkshireman' – was to follow in May 1948; this departed from Bradford Exchange at 10am and from Marylebone at 4.50pm. Comprising nine coaches usually, the train – like 'The Cutler – included a restaurant car and was hauled by an 'A3'. The 'South Yorkshireman' was allowed 5 hours 30 minutes in the down direction.

Alongside these officially named trains, there were others that had unofficial names: the 'Newspaper' left Marylebone at 1.45am and the 'Breakfast' departed from Manchester Central at 8.30am. The normal weekday service pattern was six up services from Sheffield and beyond to Marylebone and seven down. In addition, there were local services that ran, for example, from Sheffield Victoria to Nottingham Victoria or Marylebone to Woodford Halse (which was renamed from Woodford & Hinton on 1 November 1948).

In terms of motive power, ex-LNER classes – such as the 'A3s', 'B1s' and 'V2s' – dominated main-line services although as the 1950s progressed, and particularly after the line passed to LMR control, so the ubiquitous ex-LMS 'Black 5' started to appear in increasing numbers whilst the Thompson-designed Class L1 2-6-4T supplanted older designs on suburban services out of Marylebone. There were still examples of pre-Grouping classes visible but as the decade wore on, so these were gradually to disappear. From 1958 BR Standard Class 9F 2-10-0s were to become an increasing feature of freight traffic over the route and, in the years immediately before closure, diesel traction was also to appear.

The 1950s were a decade of challenge for the railways. There was the issue of catching up on the investment and maintenance missed during the wartime years. Alongside this, the growth in private car ownership and long distance coach travel, aided by improvements to the road network, ate into the railway's income. The ex-GC main line, designed as a high-speed route at the height of Victorian ambition, was ill-placed to deal with the inexorable decline of traffic as it passed through sparsely populated areas and was often in competition with alternative main line railways from the major population centres that it served.

The transfer of the line to London Midland Region in 1958 is often seen as the watershed moment when the line's fate was sealed; in reality, even if it had remained with the Eastern Region, it's hard to escape the conclusion that the line would have fallen victim to rationalisation in the 1960s given that the ex-Midland main line gave equally good access to the major towns and cities that both served – such as Leicester, Nottingham and Sheffield. With the benefit of hindsight, the loss of the ex-GC line was unfortunate given the completion of the Channel Tunnel, the renaissance in railway travel and the desire to construct a new high-speed line north from London but, in the early 1960s, none of these seemed likely. Some of the intermediate stations – such as Culworth – were to lose their passenger services in the late 1950s but it was the transfer of the through expresses that indicated that the line's long-term future was in doubt. The 'Master Cutler' was diverted to operate to King's Cross on 15 September 1958 whilst the 'South Yorkshireman' – along with the other surviving through services over the route – were to transferred or withdrawn from 2 January 1960.

Even before the publication of the Beeching report – *The Reshaping of British Railways* – in March 1963 many of the intermediate stations – such as Charwelton – had closed with the withdrawal of most of the local services; March 1963 also witnessed the demise of services via the GC's Chesterfield loop. Given the circumstances, few would have been surprised that Beeching recommended the withdrawal of all passenger services north of Aylesbury, although, in the event, the section between Rugby Central and Nottingham Victoria (later cut back to Arkwright Street) was given a temporary reprieve.

Whilst passenger traffic was undoubtedly the glamorous side of railway operation, the ex-GC main line also played host to a considerable amount of freight; the route's well-engineered alignment with no sharp curves – the route's minimum radius for curves was one mile – made it ideal for high-speed freight traffic. This was recognised by the LNER when they introduced fast and regular freight trains between the marshalling yard at Annesley and Woodford Halse; these trains, bringing Yorkshire steel and coal from the Midlands, were known to the professionals as 'Runners' but became popularly known to enthusiasts as 'Windcutters'. In later years, when hauled by the '9Fs' allocated to the route, these services operated at speeds similar to those achieved by passenger services.

With ministerial approval for the closure of the route, services between Aylesbury and Rugby Central and from Nottingham Victoria northwards were withdrawn on 5 September 1966. The surviving service was cut back from Victoria to Arkwright Street in Nottingham on 4 September 1967 to permit the demolition of Victoria station and the site's redevelopment. The remaining passenger services – from Rugby to Arkwright Street – by now operated by DMU were withdrawn of 5 May 1969.

This was not quite the end of the story, however. The section of line north from Aylesbury to Calvert survives as a freight route; indeed passenger services have been reinstated for a slight distance north of Aylesbury to a new station Aylesbury Vale Parkway. The section from Loughborough Central to a new station Leicester North is the preserved Great Central. North of Loughborough – and soon to be rejoined to the original preserved section once the bridge over the Midland main line has been reconstructed – is the line though East Leake to Ruddington. Again initially retained for freight traffic after the route's closure to passenger services, this is now also preserved and, eventually, it will be possible

to travel from Leicester to the southern outskirts of Nottingham over a revitalised GC main line.

Elsewhere there are tantalising glimpses of the lost route; although much of the route through Leicester has been demolished, the wide viaduct on which Leicester Central stood still survives and is subject to a restoration scheme, whilst elsewhere, for example, it is still possible to identify the line's route to the west of the M1 to the south of Leicester. Sadly, the destruction of Brackley viaduct and the loss of the trackbed elsewhere makes it unlikely that the route can ever be wholly recreated but the choice of route for the planned HS2 indicates perhaps how strong was Sir Edward Watkins's original vision.

The southern terminus of the Great Central main line was Marylebone station in London. Designed by Henry William Braddock, the relatively modest station was completed in a revival of the Wren style of the late 17th century and was constructed in brick and stone. The station opened to passenger services on 15 March 1899 and comprised four platforms although the original design had envisaged eight (with the remaining four to be added latter as traffic developed). Linked to the station by an extension to the Porte Cochère – but developed by a separate company as a result of the costs involved in the construction of the London Extension – was the Great Central Hotel. This was converted into offices in 1945 and, as 222 Marylebone Road, was famous as the site of the headquarters of BR between 1948 and 1986; it was reconverted into a hotel in 1993. This view from the west in the mid-1950s shows the façade of the station with taxis awaiting their next passengers. *Julian Thompson/Online Transport Archive*

On 18 August 1951 Class V2 2-6-2 No 60845 is seen reversing out of one of the platform roads at Marylebone as the empty stock it brought into the station on a southbound express is shunted in the background. Gresley's versatile design of mixed traffic locomotive were regular performers on the ex-GC main line and, when recorded here, No 60845 was allocated to Woodford Halse. In all 184 of the 'V2' class were constructed between June 1936 and July 1944; No 60845 was completed at Darlington in February 1939. *Julian Thompson/Online Transport Archive*

Gresley's successor as CME of the LNER was Edward Thompson; amongst the locomotive designs he produced for the company was the 'L1' 2-6-4T. Produced primarily for suburban services into King's Cross and Marylebone, 100 of the type were constructed in 1945 – when the prototype was completed – and between 1948 and 1950. Neasden-allocated No 67756 is seen here about to draw the empty stock from a southbound service out of the station.

No 67756 was built originally by North British and new in December 1948; with the run-down in steam in the London area, all of the 'L1' class were withdrawn between 1960 and the end of 1962. *Julian Thompson/Online Transport Archive*

To the north of Marylebone station, slightly beyond the Rossmore Road bridge, was a turntable and, on 19 April 1952, Class B1 No 61187 is seen being turned. With a total of 410 being constructed between 1942 and 1950, the 'B1' class was largest single type of Thompson's designs for the LNER. No 61187, built at Vulcan Foundry in July 1947, was at this date allocated to Leicester. *Julian Thompson/Online Transport Archive*

Class A3 Pacific No 60059 *Tracery* speeds through Neasden South on 27 September 1952 with a down service from Marylebone to Manchester. The locomotive, which was based at King's Cross for much of its career after World War 2, was allocated to Leicester between March 1951 and April 1957. New originally as LNER No 2558 in March 1925, the locomotive was converted to 'A3' in July 1942. Fitted with a double chimney in July 1958, No 60059 was to receive smoke deflectors in September 1961, just over a year before withdrawal (in December 1962).
*Neil Davenport/Online Transport Archive*

In June 1966 'Black 5' No 44941 enters Chalfont & Latimer station with a down service towards Nottingham. Built at Horwich in December 1945, the locomotive was approaching the end of its life when recorded here; it was to be withdrawn from Colwick Shed in November 1966.
*Geoffrey Tribe/Online Transport Archive*

On 12 August 1961 – a year after the withdrawal of express services over the line – 'B1' class 4-6-0 No 6110 pauses at Stoke Mandeville with a service from Woodford Halse to Marylebone. The section of the route from Chalfont & Latimer to Aylesbury Town station was opened by the Metropolitan Railway on 1 September 1892 and, following the completion of the GC's London Extension, was to be jointly controlled by the Great Central and Metropolitan railways. Following the closure of the line north of Aylesbury, the section south remained open for suburban services into Marylebone. No 61120 was one of the class to be constructed by North British in Glasgow and entered service in January 1947. *Neil Davenport/Online Transport Archive*

Gresley-designed 'V2' 2-6-2 No 60879 has the road at Aylesbury on 2 August 1958 with an up service towards Marylebone. The signalling at the south end of Aylesbury station was controlled by Aylesbury South box, which had been opened in June 1908 as part of the resignalling for the joint GC/GW station. The box was to close on 24 November 1990, when the semaphore signalling was replaced by colour lights, and, early the following year, was moved, with its frame, for storage on the preserved Great Central. Re-erected to control Swithland Sidings, the restored box was opened in May 2012. No 60879 was constructed at Doncaster in August 1940 and was to survive until withdrawal in December 1962. *Marcus Eavis/Online Transport Archive*

Views looking towards the north, 'B1' 4-6-0 No 61141 awaits departure from Aylesbury with an up service towards Marylebone in 1959. In the background can be seen the small two-road engine shed that the GWR constructed in 1893. This structure replaced an earlier shed, located to the south of the station, that had been opened by the Wycombe Railway following the opening of the branch from Princes Risborough; this had been extended in 1871. The 1893 shed was to close on 16 June 1962 and was demolished. No 61141 was the second of the class to be constructed at Vulcan Foundry and entered service in April 1947.
*Marcus Eavis/Online Transport Archive*

It's 13 August 1966 and through services on the ex-GC main line are now approaching their withdrawal as 'Black 5' No 45289 awaits departure from Aylesbury with the 4.38pm service from Marylebone to Nottingham Victoria. Although passenger services north of Aylesbury ceased on 5 September 1966, the section north of Aylesbury to Calvert was retained for freight traffic connecting into the ex-LNWR Oxford to Bletchley line via the wartime spur built between the two lines. On 14 December 2008 services to Aylesbury were extended slightly to the north to serve a new station, Aylesbury Vale Parkway.
*Marcus Eavis/Online Transport Archive*

On 3 September 1966 – the last Saturday of the GC's London Extension – 'Black 5' No 44872 is seen passing through Quainton Road station with an up service towards Marylebone. Quainton Road was originally an intermediate station on the Aylesbury & Buckingham Railway, later Metropolitan Railway, through to Verney Junction on the LNWR's line from Oxford to Cambridge and opened on 23 September 1868. The opening of the GCR London Extension resulted in the station being relocated to the east of the road overbridge visible in the distance with the actual junction between the two lines being to the west. Quainton Road was also the terminus of the Brill Tramway, which operated between 1871 and 1935. Passenger services over the section to Verney Junction, operated by the Metropolitan Railway's successor – the London Passenger Transport Board – ceased on 6 July 1936 when LPTB services ceased to operate north of Aylesbury. Quainton Road had lost its remaining passenger services on 4 March 1963 before the final closure of the London Extension. Although freight wagons are visible to the right of the train, freight facilities at the station had also been officially withdrawn by closure (on 4 July 1966). Following the withdrawal of passenger services, the line between Quainton Road and the wartime connection to the Oxford-Cambridge line was retained for freight traffic whilst the station and yard were developed into the Buckinghamshire Railway Museum. *Martin Jenkins/Online Transport Archive*

The last station on the London Extension before it connected into the Metropolitan line south through Aylesbury was Calvert and, on 9 May 1959, 'K3/2' No 61843 enters the station with the 5pm service from Marylebone to Woodford Halse. Slightly to the north of the station a spur was opened, on 14 September 1940, to provide a connection through to the ex-LNWR Oxford to Bletchley line; this was designed to permit traffic to be diverted from the original Metropolitan line from Quainton Road to Verney Junction. Calvert was one of the intermediate stations closed with the withdrawal of local passenger services over the London Extension on 4 March 1963; freight facilities were to last a further 12 months, before withdrawal on 4 May 1964. Although the station buildings at Calvert have been demolished, the island platform remains and freight traffic still passes through. With the development of the revived Oxford to Cambridge corridor, the possibility of extending passenger services north from the existing terminus at Aylesbury Vale Parkway was under consideration but the station is also on the alignment of the planned HS2 north of London. No 61843 was one of 183 of Gresley's design of 2-6-0 to be built between 1923 and 1937 following on from the first 10 constructed for the GNR. New in February 1925 and built at Darlington, No 61843 was withdrawn in August 1961. *Mike Mitchell/Transport Treasury*

One of the most significant engineering works on the London Extension was the viaduct slightly to the south of Brackley. When work commenced on the construction of the viaduct the contractor for the work – Walter Scott & Co of Newcastle – was warned about the unstable nature of the land towards the southern end but this only became apparent with the viaduct approaching completion when cracks started to appear. As a result the two southernmost arches were replaced by steel girders and the second pier was strengthened – as is evident in this view of the viaduct take in the later summer of 1966 contemporaneously with the line's closure. The viaduct was to survive intact until, despite opposition, it was demolished in 1978 to provide hard core for road construction in Milton Keynes.
*Marcus Eavis/Online Transport Archive*

It's Saturday 3 September 1966 and the final obsequies for the London Extension are imminent with through services north of Aylesbury ceasing that day (with the line being officially closed as from the following Monday – the 5th). Pictured heading northbound at Brackley Central is Type 2 (later Class 24) No D5000. Freight facilities had been withdrawn from the station on 14 June 1965 and there has already been considerable rationalisation of the track since the withdrawal.
*Martin Jenkins/Online Transport Archive*

Passengers wait on the platform at Brackley Central as 'V2' 2-6-2 No 60967 draws into the station with a southbound service in the summer of 1963. No 60967 was completed at Darlington Works in March 1943 and, when recorded here, was approaching the end of its operational career; it was to be withdrawn in February 1964. Brackley Central closed with the line north of Aylesbury on 5 September 1966 and the platform buildings were soon demolished although the main building, constructed on the road overbridge, remains in commercial use and has recently been converted into a café. The old good shed, however, still does survive having been refurbished for commercial use as part of an industrial estate. Today it is somewhat anachronistically called 'The Engine Shed'. *Marcus Eavis/Online Transport Archive*

On 3 July 1963 'Black 5' No 45444 awaits departure from Brackley Central with a northbound service. New in December 1937, the locomotive was one of the class constructed at the Newcastle works of Sir W. G. Armstrong Whitworth & Co Ltd.
*Paul de Beer/Online Transport Archive*

Pictured at the head of the 4.38pm service from Marylebone to Nottingham Victoria during the last summer of through services over the GC main line, 'Black 5' No 44858 is seen near Brackley with four coaches heading northbound.
*Marcus Eavis/Online Transport Archive*

On 11 June 1962 'B1' No 61138 heads southbound into Helmdon station with the 1.5pm stopping service from Woodford Halse to Marylebone. A typical London Extension station – with its island platform and station building on the road overbridge at the southern end – Helmdon lost its passenger services when the stopping services were withdrawn on 4 March 1963. The freight traffic to the small goods yard – primarily coal – was to survive until 2 November 1964. The station buildings were demolished in 1966 but there are still traces of the platform and the trackbed both north and south of the station is still intact; the section south is now in use as a footpath. There was a second station serving Helmdon; this was situated on the Stratford-upon-Avon & Midland Junction Railway but this had closed on 2 July 1951. The SMJR passed below the London Extension slightly to the north of the GC station as the main line crossed the short Helmdon Viaduct.
*Mike Mitchell/Transport Treasury*

A number of intermediate stations on the London Extension were closed in the late 1950s; one of those to lose its services was Culworth, where passenger and general freight traffic were both withdrawn on 29 September 1958 although the coal yard continued in operation until 4 June 1962. On 17 August 1963, 'Royal Scot' No 46122 *Royal Ulster Rifleman* passes the long-closed station with the 5.15pm service from Nottingham Victoria to Marylebone. Although the station buildings and platform at Culworth have been subsequently demolished, with the site occupied by farm building, both the goods shed and stationmaster's house remain extant in private ownership.
No 46122 had originally been built by North British in October 1927 to a design by Fowler; following Stanier's introduction of the rebuilt version of the class with taper boiler, double chimney and new cylinders in 1943, No 46122 was rebuilt in April 1948. It was to survive until October 1964. *Mike Mitchell/Transport Treasury*

Pictured passing Culworth on 14 May 1966 with the 2.38pm service from Marylebone to Nottingham is 'Black 5' No 45190. This was one of the class of Stanier's 4-6-0s constructed by Sir W. G. Armstrong Whitworth & Co Ltd and was new in October 1935. *Mike Mitchell/Transport Treasury*

On 9 August 1959 the RCTS (London Branch) organised the 'Grafton' rail tour which departed from King's Cross and travelled via Hitchin, Bedford and Northampton to Blisworth for a trip westwards over the Stratford-on-Avon & Midland Junction line to Byfield. From Byfield, the special travelled to Woodford Halse where it reversed for a trip south over the GC main line as far as Calvert Junction where it again reversed to head for Verney Junction. Motive power for the section from Blisworth to Verney Junction was provided by 'Black 5' No 45091 and the train is seen here, with the locomotive having run round, prior to its departure southbound.
*Neil Davenport/Online Transport Archive*

With the now derelict shed at Woodford Halse lying in the background, 'Black 5' No 45292 with a northbound service is recorded from a slightly unorthodox location on 3 September 1966, two days before the official closure of the line north of Aylesbury on Monday the 5th. Although the shed at Woodford Halse had originally been constructed by the GCR, it had been rebuilt by the Eastern Region prior to the transfer of control to the LMR. The shed was officially closed on 14 June 1965 and was subsequently demolished; the site of the shed is now occupied by an industrial estate. *Martin Jenkins/Online Transport Archive*

As a result of its generous loading gauge, it was possible regularly to see locomotives from the Western Region operating over the GC on inter-regional services to and from the south of England. On 27 May 1961 'Hall' class No 6929 *Underley Hall* is seen passing through Charwelton with the 11.16am service from Bournemouth to York. No 6929 was one of a number of the Collett-designed 'Hall' class to be constructed during World War 2; it was completed at Swindon in November 1941. It was destined to survive until withdrawal in October 1963. Charwelton lost its passenger services with the withdrawal of local trains over the GC route on 4 March 1963. From the goods yard, and visible in the foreground, was a two-mile branch that served local ironstone quarries; traffic from this continued for sometime after public freight facilities had been withdrawn from the station – on 4 March 1963 as well – and in its heyday it was possible to see 200 wagons or more is the sidings. *Mike Mitchell/Transport Treasury*

Two years later – on 25 May 1963 – inter-regional services still run over the London Extension but the motive power has changed. Replacing the 'Hall' at Charwelton with the northbound service from Bournemouth to York is English Electric Type 3 (later Class 37) No D6800; at this date the diesel-electric was virtually brand-new, having been completed at Vulcan Foundry in December 1962. *Mike Mitchell/Transport Treasury*

An unidentified Gresley-design Class V2 2-6-2 passes through Braunston & Willoughby on 8 July 1961 with an up service to Marylebone. By this date the London Extension was living on almost borrowed time; on 4 January 1960 through services over the line to Bradford, Manchester and Sheffield were withdrawn, being replaced by three semi-fast services per day between Marylebone and Nottingham Victoria. Deemed a duplicate route in the *Reshaping* report of March 1963, stopping services over the route had been withdrawn before the publication of Beeching's proposals and the report advocated the withdrawal of the remaining services north of Aylesbury.
*Mike Mitchell/Transport Treasury*

Seen heading north through the already closed Braunston & Willoughby station on 8 July 1961 is 'B1' class No 61028 with the 8.10am inter-regional service from Swansea to York.
*Mike Mitchell/Transport Treasury*

Two stations served Braunston. The ex-LNWR Braunston London Road closed with the line from Weedon to Leamington on 15 September 1958 whilst Braunston & Willoughby on the GC main line was already closed by that date (on 1 April 1957). When seen here on 8 July 1961 with 'Black 5' No 45223 heading northbound with the 12.25pm service from Marylebone to Nottingham the station was still largely intact; the buildings and platform were largely demolished during 1961 and 1962. Although much of the trackbed – including the bridge over the A45 – has disappeared, the stationmaster's house is still extant and is now in private ownership.
*Mike Mitchell/Transport Treasury*

Pictured passing the water tower to the south of Rugby Central with the up 'South Yorkshireman' in early 1953 is Leicester (38C) allocated Class A3 Pacific No 60107 *Royal Lancer*. The locomotive, which was one of the earliest of Gresley's Pacifics to be built (at Doncaster in May 1923), had originally been LNER No 4476 and had initially been allocated the number 506 under the first 1946 renumbering (although was never physically to carry that number) before becoming No 107 in October 1946. When recorded here, the locomotive had been recently outshopped in BR green, having carried BR blue until December 1952. The locomotive was to be fitted with a double chimney in June 1959 and smoke deflectors in

February 1962. No 60107 was withdrawn from Grantham in September 1963. The 'South Yorkshireman' was a named service introduced by BR in May 1948 to link Bradford Exchange with Marylebone; the up service departed from Bradford at 10am with the down departing from London at 4.50pm. It was routed from Bradford via Halifax and Huddersfield to Sheffield and then over the GC main line. With the withdrawal of through services over the GC main line as from 4 January 1960, the 'South Yorkshireman' was replaced by a new service from Bradford Forster Square, incorporating coaches from Halifax at Sheffield Midland, to St Pancras. *John McCann/Online Transport Archive*

One of Edward Thompson's 'B1' class 4-6-0s heads south through Rugby Central with an up service during the spring of 1953. No 61153 was another of the class completed at Vulcan Foundry, in May 1947, and was to survive in service until January 1965.
*John McCann/Online Transport Archive*

Also heading south, but over a year later in the late summer of 1954, is Class J11 0-6-0 No 64327 hauling a rake that includes both a six-wheel and a four-wheel van. Designed by John Robinson, who was the Great Central's Chief Mechanical Engineer between 1900 and 1922, 174 of the class were constructed between 1901 and 1910 by a variety of manufacturers, including Neilson Reid & Co Ltd, Vulcan Foundry and the GC's own workshops at Gorton.

No 64327 was one of those completed at Neilsen Reid, in November 1902. Although the class was intact at the start of 1953, the first withdrawals occurred during that year and No 64327 was itself to succumb in January 1957. The last of the class were withdrawn by the end of 1961; none survive in preservation. *John McCann/Online Transport Archive*

Another GWR design is seen on a down inter-regional service as 'Modified Hall' No 7911 *Lady Margaret Hall* passes through Lutterworth station with the 11.16am from Bournemouth to Newcastle on 21 July 1961. The 'Modified Hall' class represented an update by Hawksworth to the original Collett design and the first of the class entered service in March 1944. No 7911 was one of those constructed post-Nationalisation, being completed at Swindon in February 1950. The last of the class – No 7929 *Wyke Hall* – was completed nine months later. As a relatively late locomotive No 7911 was destined to have a short operational career, being finally withdrawn in December 1963 – one of the earlier of the 'Modified Halls' to be taken out of service. Lutterworth station was one of the intermediate stations closed with the final withdrawal of the Rugby to Nottingham service on 5 May 1969. The station was subsequently demolished and the site is now occupied by a housing estate.
*Mike Mitchell/Transport Treasury*

Pictured about three miles north of Lutterworth station with a down freight are Class 9F Nos 92073 and 92091 on 17 August 1960. Construction of the M1 north of Rugby resulted in the motorway running parallel to and to the east of the ex-Great Central line north from Lutterworth to a point just south of Leicester. The trackbed of this section is still identifiable whilst the bridge constructed to carry the railway over the new motorway – which ultimately had an operational life of barely four years – between Cosby and Whetstone still passes over the motorway. *Mike Mitchell/Transport Treasury*

Pictured in 1956 when brand-new, BR Standard Class 5MT No 73158 heads into Ashby Magna station with a down service towards Nottingham. Slightly to the south of the station was the short Ashby Tunnel – only 88 yards in length – that passed under the minor road from Dunton Bassett to Gilmorton. Ashby Magna station attracted a reasonable number of passengers and so was to survive through until the final withdrawal of passenger services on the Rugby to Nottingham section on 5 May 1969. The trackbed of the railway is still largely extant through Ashby Magna although the rural backdrop visible in this view is no more as the M1 motorway now runs parallel to the now-closed railway. No 73158 – one of 172 of the type constructed between April 1951 and May 1957 – was completed at Doncaster Works in December 1956; like many of the BR Standard types, it was destined to have a relatively short operational life, being withdrawn in October 1967.
*Mike Mitchell/Transport Treasury*

Some seven years later – on 9 August 1963 – a second BR Standard, this time Class 4 2-6-0 No 76086, departs from Ashby Magna with the 6.15pm service from Nottingham to Rugby. This view, taken towards the north shows to good effect the typical station design of the London Extension: an island platform with platform buildings and the main station building situated on the road overbridge. The station was demolished after closure – although traces of the platform can still be seen – and, although the bridge on Station Road is still extant, it has been infilled, thereby burying the station lamp room that once existed beneath the bridge. No 76086 was built at Horwich in May 1957; it was to see less than a decade of service before withdrawal in September 1966. *Mike Mitchell/Transport Treasury*

Heading passed milepost 104, to the south of Leicester Central station, with an up freight is Class 9F 2-10-0 No 92013. To the east of the line here was situated the GC's Leicester shed; this facility had originally opened in 1897 and included a coaling stage, turntable and water tower. The shed was closed by BR on 31 July 1964 and was subsequently demolished. One of the earliest '9F's to be completed – at Crewe Works in May 1954 – No 92013 was destined to have a much longer working life than many of the class, not being withdrawn until September 1966.
*John Worley/Online Transport Archive*

The old and the new order alongside each other just south of the Upperton Road overbridge in Leicester are a virtually brand-new Type 3 (later Class 37) and a more care-worn 'Black 5'. In the background can be seen the wagon repair shops that served Leicester North goods shed; more than 50 years after the date of the photograph – March 1965 – this building, albeit now modified, is still extant and in commercial use being occupied by a number of retailers and a well-known chain of coffee shops. Leicester North goods was the final section of the ex-GC to survive in Leicester; occupied from 1973 by the scrap merchant Vic Berry. The scrapyard, which was operational until 1991 when a major fire effectively resulted in the site's closure, was accessed from the south via a connection into the ex-Midland route from Leicester to Burton and, between 1983 and closure, a significant number of locomotives were scrapped on the site. Since final closure, much of the infrastructure of the erstwhile main line has been demolished and the land redeveloped. Part of the trackbed is now a footpath but the area to the south of the demolished overbridge between the trackbed and the wagon repair shops is now occupied by student accommodation and a supermarket.
*John Worley/Online Transport Archive*

On 24 July 1961 another of the BR Standard Class 5MT 4-6-0s – No 73159 – approaches Rothley station with the 8.40am service from Marylebone to Nottingham. One of the intermediate stations closed with the withdrawal of stopping services on 4 March 1963, it is still possible to catch trains from Rothley as it is now one of the intermediate stations on the preserved Great Central Railway.

The station – which was never supplied with electricity prior to its closure by BR – is still lit by gas and has been restored to the condition in which it existed in the years immediately before World War 1 (although electricity is now available as well).
*Mike Mitchell/Transport Treasury*

On the same day the 9.55am stopping service from Rugby to Nottingham pulls into Rothley station behind Thompson-designed Class L1 2-6-4T No 67747. Designed primarily for use on suburban services into King's Cross and Marylebone, the first of the class emerged in 1945 but it was not until 1948 that further examples were constructed. Between January 1948 and September 1950 a further 99 were completed, with work shared between Darlington Works, North British and Robert Stephenson & Hawthorns Ltd. No 67747 was one of those completed at North British – in December 1948 – but, like the remainder of the class, was destined to have a relatively short life, being withdrawn in July 1962 as their duties were gradually taken over by DMUs. All of the class had been withdrawn by the end of 1962.
*Mike Mitchell/Transport Treasury*

The 9.25am service from Nottingham to Leicester pulls into Quorn & Woodhouse station behind 'B1' class 4-6-0 No 61085 on 24 July 1961. The locomotive, completed at North British in October 1946, was approaching the end of its career when recorded here; it was withdrawn five months later. Like Rothley, Quorn & Woodhouse lost its passenger services on 4 March 1963 but is today served by trains operated by the preserved Great Central Railway. The station building is now Grade 2 listed although the signalbox that controls the station is not original; it was relocated from the MS&L station at Market Rasen and was first constructed in 1890.
*Mike Mitchell/Transport Treasury*

On 14 October 1962 the LCGB organised the 'Midland Limited' excursion from Marylebone for a tour of lines in the East Midlands. For the section from London to Nottingham Victoria, the special employed 'B16' class 4-6-0 No 61438. Originally built at Darlington Works to a design of Vincent Raven in February 1923, this was one of seven of the class to be rebuilt by Gresley between 1937 and 1940 with Walschaert valve gear, higher running plates and extended smokeboxes. These seven, designated Class B16/2, along with the 17 modified by Thompson – the Class B16/3 – were to outlive the unmodified examples, with the last being withdrawn in 1964. No 61438 was finally to be withdrawn in June 1964.
*Leslie R. Freeman/Transport Treasury*

On 8 September 1962, 'Britannia' class Pacific No 70014 *Iron Duke* heads north from Loughborough Central with the 5.15pm service from Leicester Central to Nottingham Victoria. A handful of this class were allocated – briefly – to Annesley shed in 1962; alongside Nos 70014, 70015, 70048 and 70049, which were transferred there in June, No 70043 was based at Annesley between February and June the same year. All were transferred away from the ex-Great Central route by the end of the year, with No 70014 heading for Llandudno Junction.
*Mike Mitchell/Transport Treasury*

Heading an up freight near Loughborough on 18 April 1964 is 2-10-0 No 92021. This was one of 10 of the batch – Nos 92020-29 – that were originally fitted with Franco-Crosti boilers when new in 1955. The boiler was designed in the 1930s by Attilio Franco and Dr Piero Crosti. The main difference between it and conventional feedwater heaters is that it used both exhaust steam and exhaust gases from the firebox. Conventional feedwater heaters only use exhaust steam. With the modified 2-10-0s, the chimney was retained, but was only used for lighting-up and was blanked when running. The final chimney was located on the right-hand side, just forward of the firebox. The preheaters provided less improvement than had been expected in fuel consumption and were a problem for maintenance, as a result of acidic flue gases condensing in the feedwater heater and causing corrosion. As a result all 10 were converted to conventional format between 1959 and 1962 although they all retained the pre-heat boiler – sealed off – beneath the main boiler, which resulted in them possessing a smaller boiler than that fitted to the normal '9Fs'.
*Mike Mitchell/Transport Treasury*

The 2.38pm service from Marylebone to Nottingham is pictured again, this time on 22 August 1964 as 'Black 5' No 44665 – one of these completed after Nationalisation (by Crewe Works in June 1949) – ascends the gradient out of Loughborough Central towards Barnston Box tunnel.
*Mike Mitchell/Transport Treasury*

On 12 February 1958 the photographer's shadow highlights the low winter sun as Class 01 2-8-0 No 63886 heads an up freight south of East Leake. Designed originally by Robinson for the GC and designated Class 9K, the type was constructed primarily for coal traffic. Proving to be highly successful, the design was later adopted by the Railway Operating Division of the Royal Engineers for military use during World War 1 with more than 500 being constructed between 1917 and 1919. A total of 329 of the type passed to BR in 1948; of these the majority were designated O4 (with various sub-classes based on modifications) whilst a number – including No 63886 – were designated Class O1, having been rebuilt to the design of Edward Thompson after 1944. In all, 58 were to be rebuilt between then and the end of 1950 with No 63886 being modified in November 1948. The modified locomotives included 'B1' type boilers, side-window cabs, raised running plates and Walschaert valve gear. No 63886 was to survive until November 1961 but the last 'O1' was not withdrawn until 1965. One of the original locomotives No 63601 – designated Class O4/1 – survives in preservation.
*Mike Mitchell/Transport Treasury*

The evening shadows lengthen on 14 June 1957 as Class K3/2 No 61850 heads into East Leake station with a southbound freight. The first 10 of Gresley's design of 2-6-0 entered service prior to the creation of the LNER in 1923; these were to become the 'K3/1' class. After the Grouping, a further 183 were constructed; No 61850 was built by Darlington Works in March 1925; it was to survive for more than 36 years before withdrawal in June 1961. East Leake station was to retain its passenger services until 5 May 1969 although the line through the station was retained after the withdrawal of the Rugby to Nottingham services for freight to Ruddington and to the quarry at Hotchley Hill. The section of line between Loughborough and Ruddington is now operated by the Great Central (Nottingham) Ltd and so passenger trains once again pass East Leake station; although the platform remains – the buildings themselves have been demolished – lack of car parking and other issues mean that these services do not call at East Leake. *Mike Mitchell/Transport Treasury*

It's 19 June 1957 and the Eastern Region's era of controlling the London Extension is coming towards the end as Robinson-designed Class A5 4-6-2T No 69809 is seen approaching Ruddington with the 7.45pm service from Nottingham Victoria to Leicester Central. Immediately south of Ruddington station, a large military ordnance depot was established in 1940. Connected to the London Extension by a short branch, the site continued in military use – still served by rail – until 1983 and the surviving railway infrastructure was then incorporated into the Nottingham Transport Heritage Centre. The 'A5' class was originally conceived for use on suburban services out of Marylebone and 31 were built at Gorton between 1911 and 1923 with a further 13 constructed following modification to the design by Gresley at Hawthorn Leslie & Co during 1925 and 1926. A total of 43 passed to BR in 1948. No 69809 was constructed in October 1912 and was to survive until May 1959. All of the class were withdrawn by the end of 1960. *Mike Mitchell/Transport Treasury*

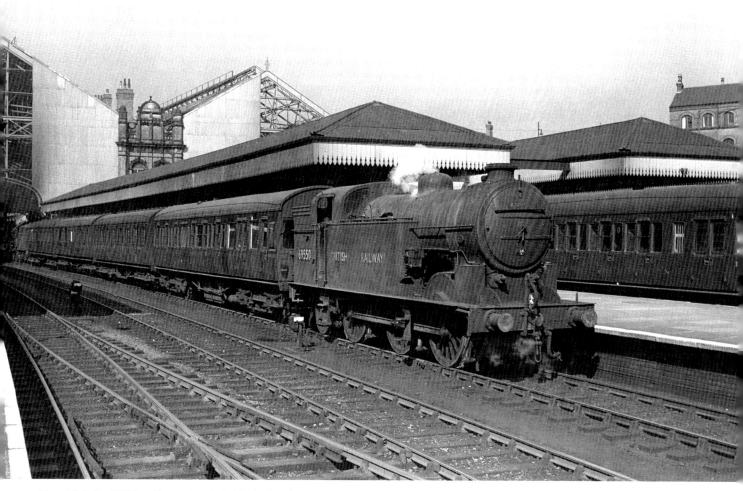

Class N2/2 No 69550 – allocated to Colwick shed at the time – is pictured at Nottingham Victoria looking towards the north and the substantial station building, designed by Albert Edward Lambert, provided by the GC for its London Extension. The station was shared between the GC and Great Northern; due to the failure of the two railways to agree on a name, the suffix 'Victoria' was suggested by the town clerk as the date of the station's proposed opening coincided with the queen's birthday. The 'N2/2' 0-6-2T was a development of Sir Nigel Gresley's earlier 'N2' – first introduced in 1920 on the GNR – and No 69550 was the first of the 'N2/2' type to be completed in 1925. Built by Beyer Peacock in Manchester, No 69550 was destined to be withdrawn in September 1958.

*D. Kelk/Online Transport Archive*

Gresley-designed Class J6 0-6-0, No 64194, stands awaiting departure in Nottingham Victoria as a photographer engages in conversation with the footplate crew. The locomotive was one of a class of 110 built at Doncaster between August 1911 and September 1922. Constructed originally in December 1912, No 64194 was one of the first examples of the type to be withdrawn in service, succumbing in November 1955 – one of three to be taken out of service that year. All were withdrawn by the end of 1962.

*D. Kelk/Online Transport Archive*

Pictured just after arriving at Nottingham Victoria station at the head of the down 'Master Cutler' on 29 July 1958 is Class 9F 2-10-0 No 92164. Contemporary reports of the locomotive's performance on the nine-coach train suggest that No 92164 achieved the 23.4 mile journey start to stop in 23.2 minutes, covering some 17½ miles at an average of 77mph with a maximum speed of some 86mph being achieved near Ruddington.
*John McCann/Online Transport Archive*

Seen approaching Nottingham Victoria from the north is No 61162 heading past the signalbox having just emerged from Mansfield Road Tunnel. On the platform some young enthusiasts watch the train arrive whilst, on the down platform, Class K3/2 No 61856 awaits departure with a northbound service. No 61162 was another of the class completed at Vulcan Foundry in May 1947; it was to survive until December 1964. Although the site of Nottingham Victoria station was largely cleared following its closure, the south portal of Mansfield Road Tunnel remains extant behind the modern shopping centre, albeit now gated to prevent access. *John McCann/Online Transport Archive*

The exterior of Nottingham Victoria station recorded in the late summer of 1965, about a year before through services over the ex-GC route were withdrawn. The station was designed by the Nottingham-based architect Albert Edward Lambert, who was also to be involved in the redesign of the competing Nottingham Midland station in the early 20th century. The construction of Victoria station was a massive undertaking. Occupying a site of some 13 acres in the city centre, work involved the demolition of 1,300 houses, 24 pubs and one church as well as the excavation of 600,000 cubic yards of sandstone. Shared between the Great Central and Great Northern railways, the new station was opened on 24 May 1900, a year after services over the GC's extension commenced, with no ceremony as the 1.12am service from Manchester to Marylebone called. Following the withdrawal of through services over the line, Victoria remained open as the northern terminus of the diesel service that operated south to Rugby Central; however, this was to cease on 4 September 1967 when services were curtailed to terminate at a reopened Arkwright Street. Following closure, the station, with the exception of the distinctive clock tower, was demolished and the site redeveloped as the Victoria Shopping Centre.
*Marcus Eavis/Online Transport Archive*

On 13 May 1962 the East Midlands branch of the RCTS organised the 'East Midlander No 5' rail tour from Nottingham Victoria to Darlington for a visit around the works. The train was double-headed from Nottingham Victoria by the unusual combination of a Southern 'Schools' class No 30925 *Cheltenham*, which was to be preserved when withdrawn later in the year, and Fowler-designed LMS Class 2P 4-4-0 No 40646. Subsequently it was noted that the '2P' should not have been used for the service as its boiler ticket had expired and this must have been amongst its last duties as it was withdrawn the same month, being scrapped in December 1962. The train, seen here at Victoria to departure, was booked to leave Nottingham at 8.35am; after travelling some 138 miles, the train arrived back in Nottingham at 9.40pm – some three minutes early. *John McCann/Online Transport Archive*

Annesley shed was one of the most important to serve the GC's London Extension and opened in 1898. Constructed in brick and with six covered roads, the shed was situated on the west side of the main line and was home to a significant number of freight locomotives, many of which were employed on the famous 'Windcutter' freight service from Annesley Yard to Woodford Halse; this fast freight service, first introduced in 1947, was to survive until June 1965 and was crucial to the operation of the ex-GC main line during these years. The freights, which were generally loose coupled, were noted for their speeds – particularly when Class 9F 2-10-0s were rostered – and regularly achieved 50mph or more, thus causing little disruption to the line's passenger services. In this view, taken on 5 May 1959, at least two '9Fs' are visible, including No 92043. The shed closed on 3 January 1966 and was demolished later the same year.
*Ron Smith/Transport Treasury*

Viewed looking towards the north on 8 October 1966 – a month after the cessation of through passenger services over the ex-GC main line and more than three years after the complete closure of the station – nature is beginning to reclaim the platforms at Kirkby Bentinck station. This was a typical station on the northern section of the main line, being constructed with two side platforms with station buildings constructed in timber and brick with substantial platform canopies. Although the original building survived on the up platform survived through until closure, that on the down platform had been demolished and replaced with a somewhat more basic shelter. Following closure, the station was demolished although some limited traces of the structure remain.
*Mike Mitchell/Transport Treasury*

Viewed from a southbound train on 1 October 1960, Tibshelf Town was another typical of many of the stations constructed on the northern section of the London Extension. When built the long platform canopies extended for the full width of the platforms, but these were subsequently cut back, as shown in this view whilst the down platform was also reconstructed at some point. There was a goods shed to the south of the station but much of the local traffic was generated by Tibshelf Colliery, to the south and east of the station, that was served by two sidings off the ex-GC route; the colliery was also served by sidings off the adjacent ex-Midland line. Tibshelf Town lost its passenger services with the withdrawal of stopping services and general freight facilities were withdrawn on 4 May 1964. Although much of the line through Tibshelf was in a cutting – and was largely infilled during the early 1970s (when all traces of the station also finally disappeared) – the 5½-mile Five Pits Trail, from Grassmoor Country Park to Tibshelf Ponds, effectively runs along the course of the erstwhile GC main line. *James Harrold/Transport Treasury*

As part of its London Extension, the Manchester, Sheffield & Lincolnshire Railway also constructed a loop to serve Chesterfield in competition with the Midland Railway. The new station opened as Chesterfield – it did not gain the suffix 'Central' until 1 November 1907 – on 4 June 1892. This view, taken on 17 December 1960, shows the end of the platforms, signalbox and good shed looking in down direction. That the ex-GC station was the poor relation was emphasised in a survey of passenger traffic in August 1961 when it was shown that in one week Central station had handled 1,829 passengers – less than a tenth of the number passing through the ex-Midland station. Passenger services via the Chesterfield loop were withdrawn when local services over the GC main line ceased on 4 March 1963. Goods traffic continued to the ex-GC yard until this took ceased on 11 September 1967 although there was a private siding that continued in operation for a period thereafter. Following complete closure and demolition, the route of the closed railway through the town was used for the construction of the Chesterfield Inner Relief Road; this opened on 25 July 1985.
*James Harrold/Transport Treasury*

On the same day, 'B1' class No 61047 enters Chesterfield Central with the 1.26pm up service from Sheffield to Nottingham. The station buildings were, like many built for the MS&L, constructed in wood with the main buildings at road level, on the Infirmary Road overbridge, also constructed in wood. Of the buildings, those on the down side were demolished shortly after the withdrawal of passenger services, those on the up platform by 1971 and the entire site had been cleared by 1973 prior to the construction of the new A61.
*James Harrold/Transport Treasury*

Pictured before the installation of the overhead for the 1,500V dc Woodhead scheme, 'B1' 4-6-0 No 61159 passes Sheffield East No 4 signalbox with the up 'South Yorkshireman' during the spring of 1952. Gorton (39A) allocated No 61159 was completed at Vulcan Foundry in May 1957. The signalbox dated originally to about 1902 and was to survive operationally until closure in September 1986. Like Victoria station itself – with the exception of the station hotel – the box has been demolished since closure.
*John McCann/Online Transport Archive*

It's now June 1957 and the 1,500V dc catenary for the Woodhead scheme is now operational as Mexborough (36B) allocated 'B1' class No 61167 – another of the type constructed at Vulcan Foundry – awaits departure from Sheffield Victoria. When the Sheffield, Ashton-under-Lyne & Manchester Railway (later part of the Manchester, Sheffield & Lincolnshire Railway) originally opened in 1845, its Sheffield terminus was at Bridgehouses – slightly to the west of the site of the future Victoria – but this was superseded by the opening of the new station – designed by John Fowler – on 5 September 1851 with the opening of the through route to the east. The new station was provided with two island platforms and 400ft long platform canopies. The front of the station was rebuilt

in 1908 and further work on the station was undertaken in 1939 and 1940. The transpennine service to Manchester Piccadilly was electrified as part of the Woodhead scheme in 1954. During the 1960s much of Victoria's traffic was diverted to the ex-Midland station and the station closed on 5 May 1970 when the Manchester service was discontinued. Services on the Huddersfield to Sheffield service passed through Victoria non-stop en route to the ex-Midland station until May 1983 when the section between Sheffield and Penistone was closed and the passenger service diverted to operate via Barnsley.
*John McCann/Online Transport Archive*

On 21 September 1958 the RCTS (Sheffield Branch) organised the 'South Yorkshire No 4' rail tour that departed from Sheffield Victoria behind 'B1' No 61165 and ex-GCR 'Large Director' class 4-4-0 No 62660 Butler Henderson – which was to preserved following withdrawal in October 1960 – at 10.40am. The tour was to travel over a number of lines to the east and north of Sheffield and the train is seen here at Victoria shortly before departure. *John McCann/Online Transport Archive*